To Ru...
Happy

Love from
Georgina & Jonathan

THE ART OF THE WARRIOR:

MASTERING THE MINDSET,
TACTICS, AND STRATEGIES OF THE
WORLD'S GREATEST FIGHTERS
FOR SUCCESS IN LIFE

MELVYN C.C. VALENZUELA

© Copyright 2023 by Melvyn C. C. Valenzuela

All rights reserved.

The content contained within this book may not be reproduced, duplicated, or transmitted without direct written permission from the author or the publisher.

Under no circumstances will any blame or legal responsibility be held against the publisher, or author, for any damages, reparation, or monetary loss due to the information contained within this book; either directly or indirectly.

Legal Notice:

This book is copyright protected. This book is only for personal use. You cannot amend, distribute, sell, use, quote or paraphrase any part, or the content within this book, without the consent of the author or publisher.

Disclaimer Notice:

Please note the information contained within this document is for educational and entertainment purposes only. All effort has been executed to present accurate, up to date, and reliable, complete information. No warranties of any kind are declared, or implied Readers acknowledge that the author is not engaging in the rendering of legal, financial, medical or professional advice.

To request permissions, contact the publisher atmcvbookshop@gmail.com

EPUB: ISBN – 978-621-8303-68-3

MOBI/KINDLE: ISBN – 978-621-8303-70-6

PDF DOWNLOADABLE: ISBN – 978-621-8303-72-0

PAPERBACK: ISBN – 978-621-8303-71-3

HARDBOUND: ISBN – 978-621-8303-69-0

NEWSPRINT: ISBN – 978-621-8303-73-7

Published by: Melvyn Cecilio C. Valenzuela

Name of Publisher: Melvyn Cecilio C.Valenzuela

Address: Muntinlupa City, Philippines 1772

Contact Details: +639063603324

ABOUT YOUR RIGHTS: This book/eBook is intended for your personal use only. It does not include any other rights.

IMPORTANT LEGAL DISCLAIMER: This book is protected by international copyright law and may not be copied, reproduced, given away, or used to create derivative works without the publisher's expressed permission. The publisher retains full copyrights to this book.

The author has made every reasonable effort to be as accurate and complete as possible in the creation of this book and to ensure that the information provided is free from errors; however, the author/publisher/ reseller assumes no responsibility for errors, omissions, or contrary interpretation of the subject matter herein and does not warrant or represent at any time that the contents within are accurate due to the rapidly changing nature of the Internet.

Any perceived slights of specific persons, peoples, or organizations are unintentional.

The purpose of this book is to educate and there are no guarantees of income, sales or results implied. The publisher/author/reseller/distributor can therefore not be held accountable for any poor results you may attain when implementing the techniques or when following any guidelines set out for you in this book.

Any product, website, and company names mentioned in this report are the trademarks or copyright properties of their respective owners. The author/publisher/reseller/distributor are not associated or affiliated with them in any way. Nor does the referred product, website, and company names sponsor, endorse, or approve this product.

AFFILIATE/COMPENSATION DISCLAIMER: Unless otherwise expressly stated, you should assume that the links contained in this book may be affiliate links and either the author/publisher/reseller/distributor will earn commission if you click on them and buy the product/service mentioned in this book. However, the author/publisher/reseller/distributor disclaim any liability that may result from your involvement with any such websites/products. You should thoroughly research before buying mentioned products or services.

This constitutes the entire license agreement. Any disputes or terms not discussed in this agreement are at the sole discretion of the publisher.

Table of Contents

I. Introduction 23

  A. Definition of the warrior mindset .25

  B. Importance of developing the warrior mindset for success in life...32

    Personal Growth 33

    Relationships 34

    Business 35

    Education....................................36

    Strategies for Developing the Warrior Mindset..38

    Mindfulness 38

    Physical Training 39

    Goal Setting..40

    Self-Awareness.....................................41

    Resilience 42

    Mental Toughness................................42

C. Overview of the book...................44

II. The Foundation of the Warrior Mindset..47

Courage 48

Honor 49

Self-Discipline 50

A. Physical fitness and training.......52

Importance of Physical Fitness...52

Types of Physical Training..........53

B. Mental toughness and discipline 56

What is Mental Toughness? 57

What is Discipline? 58

The Benefits of Mental Toughness and Discipline 58

Strategies for Developing Mental Toughness and Discipline...........59

Setting specific goals:...........................59

Developing a positive mindset:............60

Developing routines and habits: 60

Practicing mindfulness and meditation: 60

Challenging oneself: 61

The Role of Mentors and Support Networks 61

C. Focus and concentration 62

What is Focus? 63

What is Concentration? 63

The Benefits of Focus and Concentration 64

Strategies for Developing Focus and Concentration 65

Eliminating distractions: 65

Setting achievable goals: 65

Practicing mindfulness: 66

Prioritizing rest and recovery: 66

The Role of Mental and Physical Health 67

D. Mindfulness and meditation 68

What is Mindfulness?...................69

What is Meditation? 69

The Benefits of Mindfulness and Meditation 70

Strategies for Incorporating Mindfulness and Meditation into Daily Life 71

    Starting small: 71

    Finding a quiet space: 71

    Using guided meditations: 72

    Experimenting with different techniques: 72

III. Key Principles of the Warrior Mindset 74

  A. Self-Discipline.............................75

  B. Resilience 75

  C. Adaptability................................76

  D. Focus..76

  E. Courage......................................77

 F. Integrity 78

 G. Perseverance 78

 A. Courage and fearlessness 80

 B. Perseverance and resilience 82

 C. Honor and integrity 84

 D. Compassion and empathy 86

 E. Adaptability and flexibility 89

IV. Applying the Warrior Mindset to Real Life 91

 A. Career and Business 92

 B. Relationships 93

 C. Health and Wellness 94

 D. Personal Growth and Development 95

V. Conclusion 96

 A. Setting and achieving goals 97

  Identify Your Goals: 97

  Break Down Your Goals into Smaller Steps: 98

Create a Plan: 98

Build Discipline: 99

Embrace Perseverance: 99

Celebrate Your Progress: 100

B. Overcoming challenges and obstacles 101

Reframe Your Perspective: 101

Stay Positive: 102

Build Resilience: 102

Embrace Adaptability: 103

Take Action: 103

C. Building strong relationships and networks 104

Practice Communication Skills: 105

Show Respect and Compassion: 105

Build Trust: 106

Seek Out Mentors and Allies: ...106

Give Back: 107

D. Pursuing excellence in all areas of life 108

Set Clear Goals: 108

Develop a Plan: 109

Cultivate a Growth Mindset: 109

Practice Continuous Improvement: 110

Prioritize Self-Care: 110

E. Making a positive impact on the world 111

Identify Your Passion and Purpose: 112

Develop Your Skills and Expertise: 112

Find Your Role: 113

Take Action: 113

Reflect and Adjust: 114

V. Tools and Techniques for Developing the Warrior Mindset 115

Physical Training: 116
Mental Training: 116
Mindfulness: 117
Journaling: 117
Coaching and Mentoring: 118
Community and Support Networks: 118
A. Visualization and affirmations ... 119
    Be specific: 121
    Use the present tense: 121
    Repeat regularly: 122
B. Mental rehearsal and preparation 123
    Be specific: 124
    Stay positive: 125
    Practice regularly: 125
    Stay flexible: 125
C. Positive self-talk and mindset shifts 126

Be aware of negative self-talk or limiting beliefs: 128

Choose empowering statements: 128

Reframe challenges as opportunities: 129

Practice regularly: 129

D. Learning from failure and setbacks 130

Take responsibility: 131

Analyze what went wrong: 131

Learn from your mistakes: 132

Reframe failure as feedback: 132

Keep moving forward: 133

E. Continuous improvement and self-reflection 134

Set goals: 134

Track progress: 135

Seek feedback: 135

Learn new skills and knowledge: 135

Reflect on your actions and thought processes: 136

VI. The Warrior Mindset in Action: Inspirational Stories and Examples...137

Nelson Mandela: 138

Serena Williams: 138

Malala Yousafzai:...........................139

Jocko Willink: 139

Bethany Hamilton:.........................140

Maya Angelou: 140

Nick Vujicic:...................................141

Tom Brady: 141

Harriet Tubman: 142

Stephen Hawking:.........................142

Oprah Winfrey:..............................143

Bruce Lee:....................................143

Helen Keller: 144

Winston Churchill: 144

Michael Jordan:.............................145

A. Historical figures and legendary warriors 146

    Miyamoto Musashi.....................146

    Sun Tzu 146

    Alexander the Great...................147

    Joan of Arc................................147

    William Wallace 147

    Spartacus..................................148

    Genghis Khan 148

    Bruce Lee 148

    Leonidas I 149

    Saladin......................................149

    Lapu-Lapu.................................149

    Gabriela Silang 150

    Andres Bonifacio.......................150

    Emilio Aguinaldo 151

- Kudaman 151
- Lam-ang 151
- Rajah Sulayman 152
- Francisco Balagtas 152
- Gregorio del Pilar 152
- Melchora Aquino 153
- Marcelo H. del Pilar 153
- Jose Rizal 154
- Apolinario Mabini 154
- Juan Luna 154
- Antonio Luna 155
- Sultan Kudarat 155
- Francisco Dagohoy 156

B. Modern-day martial artists and athletes 156

- Ronda Rousey 156
- Georges St-Pierre 157
- Anderson Silva 157

Manny Pacquiao 157
Simone Biles 158
Usain Bolt 158
Conor McGregor 159
Efren Reyes 159
Hidilyn Diaz 159
Rolando Navarette 160
Monico Puentevella 160
Rener and Ryron Gracie 161
Margarito "Ting" Toledo 161
Elorde brothers 162
Monsour Del Rosario 162
Eduard Folayang 163

C. Everyday people who have applied the warrior mindset to succeed in life 163

Henry Sy 164
Manny Villar 164

  Tony Tan Caktiong 165
  Socorro Ramos..........................165
  Teresita Sy-Coson.....................166
  Gina Lopez 166
  Nanette Medved-Po...................166
  Efren Peñaflorida.......................167
  Lea Salonga...............................167
VII. Conclusion 168
 A. Recap of key points...................170
 B. Final thoughts and advice for readers..173
 C. Call to action for developing the warrior mindset and achieving success in life................................175

I. INTRODUCTION

The world is full of challenges and obstacles that can impede our progress and prevent us from achieving our goals. However, with the right mindset, we can overcome these challenges and succeed in all areas of life. The warrior mindset is a powerful approach to life that can help us to develop the mental and emotional resilience we need to face any situation with confidence and courage.

In this book, we will explore the warrior mindset and its importance for success in life. We will examine the key principles of the warrior mindset, and discuss how they can be applied to real-life situations to achieve our goals and make a positive impact on the world. We will also provide practical tools and techniques for developing the warrior mindset, and share inspirational stories and examples of individuals who have successfully applied this approach to their own lives.

Whether you are a martial artist, athlete, business professional, or anyone seeking to develop greater mental and emotional resilience, this book is for you. By the end of this book, you will have a deep understanding of the warrior mindset and how it can help you to succeed in all areas of life. You will also have practical tools and techniques for developing this powerful mindset, and be inspired by the stories of individuals who have successfully applied it to their own lives. Let us begin our journey into the world of the warrior mindset.

A. Definition of the warrior mindset

The concept of a warrior mindset is a relatively new term used in personal development, psychology, and leadership. It is the set of beliefs, attitudes, and actions that enable individuals to face life's challenges with courage, resilience, and adaptability. This mindset is rooted in the warrior archetype that has been present in almost every culture throughout history. In this essay, I will discuss the definition of the warrior mindset, its origins, and how it can be applied in everyday life.

To begin with, the warrior mindset can be defined as the state of mind that enables individuals to face their fears, overcome obstacles, and achieve their goals with strength, focus, and discipline. It is a way of thinking that prioritizes personal responsibility, continuous improvement, and self-mastery. The warrior mindset is not limited to the martial arts or military professions. Rather, it can be applied in any domain where individuals face challenges and adversity, whether it's business, education, sports, or relationships.

The origins of the warrior mindset can be traced back to the ancient world. In many cultures, warriors were seen as the protectors of their communities, tasked with defending their people against external threats. They were trained in combat skills and mental fortitude to face the dangers of battle with courage and strength. In Japan, the samurai warriors developed a unique code of conduct known as bushido, which emphasized the virtues of loyalty, honor, and self-discipline. In the West, the Greek warriors developed the concept of arete, which referred to the pursuit of excellence in all areas of life.

Today, the warrior mindset is not limited to the military or martial arts. It has become a popular concept in personal development and leadership, where individuals seek to develop mental toughness and resilience to face life's challenges. It is often associated with the concept of grit, which refers to the perseverance and passion for long-term goals. In recent years, researchers have also studied the psychological traits of successful people, including entrepreneurs, athletes, and artists, and have found that many share the same mindset as warriors.

The warrior mindset is characterized by several key traits. The first is courage, which is the ability to face fear and take action despite it. Warriors are not fearless, but they are able to overcome their fears and act in the face of danger.

The second trait is discipline, which is the ability to maintain focus and follow through on goals and commitments. Warriors are able to stay focused on their objectives, even in the midst of chaos and distraction. The third trait is resilience, which is the ability to bounce back from setbacks and challenges. Warriors are able to adapt to change and use setbacks as learning opportunities. Finally, the warrior mindset is characterized by a strong sense of purpose and mission. Warriors have a clear vision of what they want to achieve and are driven by a sense of purpose and meaning.

One of the key benefits of developing a warrior mindset is increased confidence and self-esteem. When individuals cultivate mental toughness and resilience, they feel more capable of facing life's challenges and taking on new opportunities. They also develop a stronger sense of self-efficacy, which is the belief in one's ability to achieve their goals. This, in turn, leads to a more positive outlook on life and a greater sense of well-being.

The warrior mindset can be developed through various practices and techniques. One of the most common is the practice of mindfulness and meditation. By focusing on the present moment and observing one's thoughts and emotions without judgment, individuals can develop greater self-awareness and mental clarity. They can also learn to regulate their emotions and remain calm in stressful situations. Another practice that can help develop the warrior mindset is physical training, such as martial arts, yoga, or strength training. By pushing their bodies to the limit, individuals can develop greater physical and mental resilience.

In addition to mindfulness and physical training, the warrior mindset can also be developed through mental training techniques. Visualization and mental rehearsal are popular techniques used by athletes and performers to mentally prepare for success. By imagining oneself successfully overcoming a challenge, individuals can build confidence and motivation to take action in the real world. Another technique is positive self-talk, which involves replacing negative self-talk with positive affirmations. By focusing on one's strengths and accomplishments, individuals can develop a more positive self-image and mindset.

The warrior mindset can also be applied in various domains of life. In business, for example, individuals can develop the warrior mindset by setting ambitious goals, maintaining a strong work ethic, and staying focused on their vision despite setbacks and obstacles. In relationships, the warrior mindset can help individuals communicate more effectively, resolve conflicts, and maintain strong boundaries. In education, the warrior mindset can help students overcome academic challenges and develop a lifelong love of learning.

However, it is important to note that the warrior mindset is not without its potential drawbacks. The emphasis on personal responsibility and self-discipline can sometimes lead to a lack of empathy and understanding for others. The focus on self-improvement and goal attainment can also lead to a sense of perfectionism and burnout. It is important for individuals to balance the warrior mindset with other aspects of their lives, such as relationships, rest, and leisure.

The warrior mindset is a set of beliefs, attitudes, and actions that enable individuals to face life's challenges with courage, resilience, and adaptability. It is rooted in the warrior archetype that has been present in almost every culture throughout history. Today, the warrior mindset is not limited to the martial arts or military professions. Rather, it can be applied in any domain where individuals face challenges and adversity. By developing mental toughness, resilience, and purpose, individuals can cultivate the warrior mindset and achieve success in all areas of life. However, it is important to balance the warrior mindset with other aspects of one's life and avoid the potential drawbacks of excessive self-focus and perfectionism.

B. Importance of developing the warrior mindset for success in life

The warrior mindset is a powerful tool for success in life. It enables individuals to face life's challenges with courage, resilience, and adaptability. In this section, we will discuss the importance of developing the warrior mindset for success in various domains of life, including personal growth, relationships, business, and education.

Personal Growth

Developing the warrior mindset is essential for personal growth and self-improvement. It involves taking responsibility for one's own life and taking action to achieve one's goals.

Individuals who possess the warrior mindset are self-disciplined and committed to their personal growth. They have a strong work ethic and are willing to put in the effort necessary to achieve their goals.

The warrior mindset also involves a commitment to lifelong learning. Individuals who possess this mindset are always seeking to improve their skills, knowledge, and abilities. They are open to feedback and willing to learn from their mistakes. By embracing a growth mindset, individuals can overcome challenges and achieve success in all areas of their lives.

Relationships

The warrior mindset is also important for success in relationships. It involves effective communication, empathy, and a commitment to mutual growth and development. Individuals who possess the warrior mindset in their relationships are able to communicate effectively and resolve conflicts in a constructive manner.

They are also able to maintain strong boundaries and stand up for their own needs and values. By possessing the warrior mindset in their relationships, individuals are able to build strong and healthy relationships that are based on trust, respect, and mutual support.

Business

In the business world, the warrior mindset is essential for success. It involves setting ambitious goals, maintaining a strong work ethic, and staying focused on one's vision despite setbacks and obstacles. Individuals who possess the warrior mindset in their business endeavors are able to take risks, make tough decisions, and lead their teams to success.

They are also able to adapt to changing circumstances and remain flexible in their approach. By possessing the warrior mindset in their business endeavors, individuals are able to achieve their goals and make a positive impact in their industry.

Education

The warrior mindset is also important for success in education. It involves a commitment to lifelong learning, a growth mindset, and a willingness to overcome challenges and obstacles. Individuals who possess the warrior mindset in their education are able to embrace the learning process and overcome academic challenges.

They are also able to develop a love of learning that extends beyond the classroom. By possessing the warrior mindset in their education, individuals are able to achieve academic success and set the foundation for a successful career.

Overall, the warrior mindset is a powerful tool for success in life. It enables individuals to face life's challenges with courage, resilience, and adaptability. Whether in personal growth, relationships, business, or education, possessing the warrior mindset is essential for achieving success and making a positive impact in the world.

But how can one develop the warrior mindset? In the next section, we will discuss strategies for cultivating this powerful mindset and incorporating it into one's daily life.

Strategies for Developing the Warrior Mindset

The warrior mindset is not something that can be developed overnight. It requires a commitment to self-improvement and a willingness to face challenges and obstacles. In this section, we will discuss strategies for developing the warrior mindset and incorporating it into one's daily life.

Mindfulness

One of the most powerful strategies for developing the warrior mindset is mindfulness. Mindfulness involves being fully present in the moment and aware of one's thoughts and emotions. By practicing mindfulness, individuals can develop greater self-awareness and emotional regulation.

This can help them remain calm and focused in the face of challenges and adversity. Mindfulness can be practiced through techniques such as meditation, deep breathing, and body scan exercises.

Physical Training

Physical training is another important strategy for developing the warrior mindset. By pushing one's body to the limit, individuals can develop greater physical and mental resilience. Physical training can help individuals build strength, endurance, and discipline, all of which are essential components of the warrior mindset.

Regular exercise can also help individuals manage stress and anxiety, and improve their mood and overall well-being. In addition to traditional exercise routines, activities such as martial arts, boxing, or other combat sports can provide a unique opportunity for individuals to push themselves physically and mentally, and develop the warrior mindset.

Goal Setting

Goal setting is another important strategy for developing the warrior mindset. By setting clear and specific goals, individuals can focus their energy and efforts on achieving what they want.

This requires discipline, motivation, and a willingness to overcome obstacles.

Setting realistic goals that align with one's values and passions is key to maintaining a sense of purpose and motivation. Additionally, breaking down larger goals into smaller, more achievable steps can help individuals maintain momentum and stay on track.

Self-Awareness

Developing self-awareness is also an important strategy for cultivating the warrior mindset. By understanding one's own strengths, weaknesses, and tendencies, individuals can develop a greater sense of self-confidence and self-efficacy.

Self-awareness can be developed through various practices, including journaling, introspection, and seeking feedback from trusted friends and mentors. By becoming more aware of one's own emotions, motivations, and behavior, individuals can develop greater control over their own lives and cultivate the warrior mindset.

Resilience

Resilience is another essential component of the warrior mindset. It involves the ability to adapt to changing circumstances, overcome obstacles, and bounce back from failure or setbacks. Resilience can be developed through various practices, including exposure to challenging situations, developing a growth mindset, and seeking out support from others.

By learning to embrace challenges and setbacks as opportunities for growth and learning, individuals can cultivate greater resilience and develop the warrior mindset.

Mental Toughness

Finally, mental toughness is a critical component of the warrior mindset. It involves the ability to remain focused, disciplined, and motivated in the face of adversity. Mental toughness can be developed through various practices, including visualization, positive self-talk, and exposure to uncomfortable situations.

By learning to control one's thoughts and emotions, individuals can develop greater mental toughness and cultivate the warrior mindset.

The warrior mindset is a powerful tool for success in all areas of life. By developing greater resilience, discipline, and adaptability, individuals can overcome challenges and achieve their goals. Strategies for cultivating the warrior mindset include mindfulness, physical training, goal setting, self-awareness, resilience, and mental toughness.

By incorporating these strategies into one's daily life, individuals can develop the warrior mindset and achieve success in personal growth, relationships, business, and education. It requires a commitment to self-improvement, a willingness to face challenges, and a strong sense of purpose and passion. By embracing the warrior mindset, individuals can make a positive impact in the world and achieve their full potential.

C. Overview of the book

"The Art of the Warrior: Mastering the Mindset, Tactics, and Strategies of the World's Greatest Fighters For Success In Life" is a book that explores the principles and practices of developing the warrior mindset for success in all areas of life. The book is organized into three main sections, each focused on a different aspect of the warrior mindset.

The first section, "Understanding the Warrior Mindset," explores the origins and nature of the warrior mindset, and how it has been cultivated throughout history in various cultures and traditions. This section provides a foundational understanding of the warrior mindset, and the qualities and characteristics that define it.

The second section, "Developing the Warrior Mindset," offers practical strategies for cultivating the warrior mindset in one's own life. This section covers topics such as mindfulness, physical training, goal setting, self-awareness, resilience, and mental toughness. Each chapter includes practical exercises and tips for developing the key principles of the warrior mindset.

The final section, "Applying the Warrior Mindset," provides guidance on how to apply the warrior mindset to achieve success in various areas of life, including personal growth, relationships, business, and education. This section includes real-world examples and case studies of individuals who have successfully applied the warrior mindset to achieve their goals.

Throughout the book, the author emphasizes the importance of developing the warrior mindset as a holistic approach to success in life. The warrior mindset is not just about achieving external goals, but also about developing inner strength, resilience, and self-mastery. By cultivating the warrior mindset, individuals can become the best version of themselves and make a positive impact in the world.

Overall, "The Art of the Warrior: Mastering the Mindset, Tactics, and Strategies of the World's Greatest Fighters For Success In Life" is a comprehensive guide for anyone seeking to cultivate the qualities and characteristics of the warrior mindset. Whether you are an athlete, business professional, student, or anyone else looking to achieve your goals and fulfill your potential, this book provides practical tools and insights to help you develop the warrior mindset and achieve success in all areas of life.

II. THE FOUNDATION OF THE WARRIOR MINDSET

The foundation of the warrior mindset is rooted in the principles of courage, honor, and self-discipline. These qualities have been celebrated throughout history in various cultures and traditions, and continue to be highly valued in modern society. By understanding and embodying these foundational principles, individuals can develop the warrior mindset and achieve success in all areas of life.

COURAGE

Courage is the first foundational principle of the warrior mindset. It involves the willingness to face and overcome fear, and to take action despite potential risks and consequences. Courage is not the absence of fear, but rather the ability to act in spite of fear.

In order to develop courage, individuals must first identify their fears and understand the potential risks and benefits of taking action. They must then commit to taking action despite their fears, and be willing to face the potential consequences.

Courage is essential for success in all areas of life, from personal growth to business to relationships. Without courage, individuals may be held back by their fears and unable to achieve their full potential.

HONOR

Honor is the second foundational principle of the warrior mindset. It involves a deep sense of integrity and morality, and a commitment to doing what is right and just. Honor requires individuals to act in accordance with their values and principles, even when it is difficult or unpopular.

In order to develop honor, individuals must first identify their values and principles, and commit to living in accordance with them. They must also be willing to stand up for what is right, even in the face of opposition or adversity.

Honor is essential for success in all areas of life, as it provides a foundation of integrity and authenticity that others can trust and respect.

SELF-DISCIPLINE

Self-discipline is the third foundational principle of the warrior mindset. It involves the ability to control one's thoughts, emotions, and actions in order to achieve specific goals and outcomes. Self-discipline requires individuals to prioritize their goals and commit to taking consistent action towards achieving them.

In order to develop self-discipline, individuals must first identify their goals and develop a plan for achieving them. They must then commit to taking consistent action towards those goals, even when it is difficult or uncomfortable.

Self-discipline is essential for success in all areas of life, as it provides the necessary focus and motivation to achieve one's goals and fulfill one's potential.

By embodying the foundational principles of courage, honor, and self-discipline, individuals can develop the warrior mindset and achieve success in all areas of life. These principles provide a strong foundation of integrity, authenticity, and self-mastery that can help individuals overcome obstacles and achieve their full potential.

A. PHYSICAL FITNESS AND TRAINING

Physical fitness and training are essential components of developing the warrior mindset. By pushing their bodies to the limit, individuals can develop greater physical and mental resilience, which can be applied to all areas of life. Additionally, physical training provides an outlet for stress and anxiety, and can help individuals build self-confidence and discipline.

Importance of Physical Fitness

Physical fitness is essential for overall health and well-being, and is an important component of developing the warrior mindset. Regular exercise can improve cardiovascular health, strengthen bones and muscles, and reduce the risk of chronic diseases such as obesity, diabetes, and heart disease. Additionally, physical fitness can boost energy levels, improve mood, and reduce stress and anxiety.

Types of Physical Training

There are many types of physical training that can help individuals develop the warrior mindset. Some of the most effective forms of training include strength training, cardiovascular exercise, and martial arts.

Strength training involves lifting weights or using resistance exercises to build strength, endurance, and muscle mass. This type of training is effective for improving overall physical fitness, as well as developing mental toughness and resilience.

Cardiovascular exercise, such as running or cycling, is effective for improving cardiovascular health and endurance. This type of training is also effective for reducing stress and anxiety, and boosting mood and energy levels.

Martial arts training involves learning specific techniques and skills for self-defense and combat. This type of training is effective for developing physical and mental strength, as well as discipline, focus, and self-control.

Benefits of Physical Training

Physical training provides many benefits beyond improving physical fitness. By pushing their bodies to the limit, individuals can develop mental toughness and resilience, which can be applied to all areas of life. Physical training can also provide an outlet for stress and anxiety, and can help individuals build self-confidence and discipline.

In addition, physical training can help individuals develop a sense of purpose and direction, as they work towards specific goals and objectives. This can be especially beneficial for individuals who are struggling to find motivation or direction in their lives.

Tips for Developing a Physical Training Routine

Developing a consistent physical training routine is essential for achieving the full benefits of physical fitness. Some tips for developing a successful training routine include setting specific goals and objectives, varying the types of exercises and activities to prevent boredom, and tracking progress and results.

Additionally, it is important to stay consistent and committed to the training routine, even when it is difficult or uncomfortable. By pushing through these challenges, individuals can develop greater mental toughness and resilience, which can be applied to all areas of life.

Overall, physical fitness and training are essential components of developing the warrior mindset. By pushing their bodies to the limit, individuals can develop greater physical and mental resilience, as well as self-confidence, discipline, and a sense of purpose and direction. By incorporating physical training into their daily routines, individuals can develop the strength and resilience necessary to succeed in all areas of life.

B. MENTAL TOUGHNESS AND DISCIPLINE

Mental toughness and discipline are crucial components of the warrior mindset. These qualities enable individuals to overcome obstacles, persevere through challenges, and achieve their goals. By developing mental toughness and discipline, individuals can build resilience and confidence, and develop a sense of control over their lives.

What is Mental Toughness?

Mental toughness is the ability to remain focused, motivated, and determined in the face of adversity. It involves developing a strong mindset that is resistant to stress, anxiety, and negative self-talk. Mental toughness enables individuals to push through difficult situations and maintain their focus and motivation, even in the face of obstacles and setbacks.

What is Discipline?

Discipline involves the ability to stay committed and consistent in pursuit of one's goals. It involves developing habits and routines that support one's goals, and resisting temptations and distractions that may interfere with progress. Discipline enables individuals to stay focused and on track, even when it is difficult or uncomfortable.

The Benefits of Mental Toughness and Discipline

Mental toughness and discipline provide numerous benefits for individuals seeking to develop the warrior mindset. By cultivating these qualities, individuals can build resilience and confidence, and develop a sense of control over their lives. Additionally, mental toughness and discipline can help individuals stay focused and motivated in pursuit of their goals, even when faced with obstacles or setbacks.

Strategies for Developing Mental Toughness and Discipline

There are many strategies individuals can use to develop mental toughness and discipline. Some of the most effective strategies include:

Setting specific goals:

By setting clear, specific goals, individuals can develop a sense of purpose and direction, and stay focused on their objectives.

Developing a positive mindset:

Cultivating a positive mindset can help individuals stay motivated and focused, even in the face of challenges.

Developing routines and habits:

Establishing consistent routines and habits can help individuals stay on track and make progress towards their goals, even when motivation is low.

Practicing mindfulness and meditation:

Mindfulness and meditation can help individuals develop greater focus and resilience, and reduce stress and anxiety.

Challenging oneself:

By pushing oneself to take on new challenges and step outside of one's comfort zone, individuals can develop greater mental toughness and resilience.

The Role of Mentors and Support Networks

Developing mental toughness and discipline can be challenging, and it can be helpful to have the support of mentors and a strong network of friends and family. Mentors can provide guidance, motivation, and feedback, and can help individuals stay accountable and on track towards their goals. Support networks can provide encouragement and emotional support, and can help individuals stay motivated and engaged in their pursuits.

Overall, mental toughness and discipline are essential components of the warrior mindset. By cultivating these qualities, individuals can build resilience, confidence, and a sense of control over their lives, and can achieve their goals with greater success and satisfaction.

C. FOCUS AND CONCENTRATION

Focus and concentration are critical components of the warrior mindset. These qualities enable individuals to stay focused on their goals, resist distractions and temptations, and perform at their best, even in challenging situations. By developing focus and concentration, individuals can enhance their performance and productivity, and achieve their goals with greater success and efficiency.

What is Focus?

Focus involves the ability to concentrate one's attention and energy on a specific task or objective. It requires blocking out distractions and maintaining attention on the task at hand. Focus is a critical skill for achieving goals, as it enables individuals to stay on track and make progress towards their objectives.

What is Concentration?

Concentration involves the ability to maintain one's focus over an extended period of time. It involves sustaining one's attention and energy on a task, even when it is difficult or boring. Concentration is a key skill for success in many areas, including academics, sports, and professional pursuits.

The Benefits of Focus and Concentration

Focus and concentration provide numerous benefits for individuals seeking to develop the warrior mindset. By cultivating these qualities, individuals can enhance their performance and productivity, and achieve their goals with greater success and efficiency. Additionally, focus and concentration can help individuals stay calm and composed under pressure, and maintain their motivation and momentum towards their objectives.

Strategies for Developing Focus and Concentration

There are many strategies individuals can use to develop focus and concentration. Some of the most effective strategies include:

Eliminating distractions:

By removing distractions such as social media, phone notifications, and other interruptions, individuals can maintain their focus on the task at hand.

Setting achievable goals:

By setting clear, achievable goals, individuals can stay focused and motivated, and make progress towards their objectives.

Practicing mindfulness:

Mindfulness practices such as meditation, deep breathing, and visualization can help individuals develop greater focus and concentration.

Prioritizing rest and recovery:

Rest and recovery are critical for maintaining focus and concentration over an extended period of time. Taking breaks, getting enough sleep, and engaging in physical activity can help individuals maintain their energy and focus.

The Role of Mental and Physical Health

Mental and physical health are essential for developing and maintaining focus and concentration. Mental health conditions such as anxiety and depression can interfere with focus and concentration, and physical health issues such as chronic pain or fatigue can also impact performance. By taking care of their mental and physical health, individuals can optimize their focus and concentration and perform at their best.

In summary, focus and concentration are critical components of the warrior mindset. By cultivating these qualities, individuals can enhance their performance and productivity, achieve their goals with greater success and efficiency, and maintain their motivation and momentum towards their objectives.

D. MINDFULNESS AND MEDITATION

Mindfulness and meditation are powerful tools for developing the warrior mindset. These practices involve the cultivation of focused awareness, and can help individuals to develop greater mental clarity, emotional regulation, and resilience in the face of adversity. By incorporating mindfulness and meditation into their daily routines, individuals can develop a deeper understanding of their thoughts and emotions, and learn to respond to difficult situations with greater composure and effectiveness.

What is Mindfulness?

Mindfulness is the practice of paying attention to the present moment, without judgment. It involves bringing one's attention to the sensations of the body, the breath, and the surrounding environment, and observing one's thoughts and emotions without getting caught up in them. By practicing mindfulness, individuals can develop a greater sense of awareness and clarity, and learn to respond to challenging situations with greater skill and resilience.

What is Meditation?

Meditation is a practice that involves intentionally focusing one's attention on a specific object or sensation, such as the breath, a mantra, or an image. It is a method for training the mind to develop greater focus, clarity, and equanimity. By meditating regularly, individuals can develop greater mental and emotional resilience, and learn to respond to challenging situations with greater calm and clarity.

The Benefits of Mindfulness and Meditation

Mindfulness and meditation have numerous benefits for individuals seeking to develop the warrior mindset. By cultivating these practices, individuals can develop greater mental clarity, emotional regulation, and resilience in the face of adversity. Additionally, mindfulness and meditation can help individuals reduce stress and anxiety, improve their sleep, and enhance their overall well-being.

Strategies for Incorporating Mindfulness and Meditation into Daily Life

There are many strategies individuals can use to incorporate mindfulness and meditation into their daily routines. Some of the most effective strategies include:

Starting small:

Begin with just a few minutes of meditation or mindfulness practice each day, and gradually increase the duration as you become more comfortable with the practice.

Finding a quiet space:

Choose a quiet, comfortable space where you can focus your attention without distractions.

Using guided meditations:

Guided meditations can be helpful for beginners, as they provide a structure for the practice and help to focus the mind.

Experimenting with different techniques:

There are many different types of meditation and mindfulness practices, so it's important to find the techniques that work best for you.

The Role of Mindfulness and Meditation in the Warrior Mindset

Mindfulness and meditation are critical components of the warrior mindset, as they help individuals develop greater mental clarity, emotional regulation, and resilience. By incorporating these practices into their daily routines, individuals can develop a deeper understanding of their thoughts and emotions, and learn to respond to difficult situations with greater composure and effectiveness. Additionally, mindfulness and meditation can help individuals reduce stress and anxiety, and enhance their overall well-being, allowing them to perform at their best in all areas of life.

In summary, mindfulness and meditation are powerful tools for developing the warrior mindset. By incorporating these practices into their daily routines, individuals can develop greater mental and emotional resilience, and learn to respond to difficult situations with greater composure and effectiveness. Additionally, mindfulness and meditation can help individuals reduce stress and anxiety, and enhance their overall well-being, allowing them to perform at their best in all areas of life.

III. KEY PRINCIPLES OF THE WARRIOR MINDSET

The warrior mindset is grounded in a set of key principles that form the foundation for success in life. These principles can be applied in a variety of contexts, from physical training and martial arts, to personal and professional development. In this section, we will explore some of the key principles of the warrior mindset.

A. Self-Discipline

Self-discipline is the ability to control one's behavior and actions in order to achieve a desired goal. It requires focus, persistence, and a willingness to make sacrifices in pursuit of one's objectives. Self-discipline is a critical component of the warrior mindset, as it allows individuals to stay focused and motivated even in the face of adversity.

B. Resilience

Resilience is the ability to bounce back from setbacks and challenges. It requires mental and emotional toughness, as well as a willingness to learn from mistakes and failures. Resilience is a critical component of the warrior mindset, as it allows individuals to stay focused on their goals even in the face of adversity and uncertainty.

C. Adaptability

Adaptability is the ability to adjust to changing circumstances and situations. It requires a willingness to be flexible and to let go of preconceived notions and expectations. Adaptability is a critical component of the warrior mindset, as it allows individuals to respond effectively to changing situations and to remain focused on their goals in the midst of uncertainty.

D. Focus

Focus is the ability to concentrate one's attention on a specific task or objective. It requires mental clarity and the ability to tune out distractions and external stimuli. Focus is a critical component of the warrior mindset, as it allows individuals to stay on track and to pursue their goals with determination and purpose.

E. Courage

Courage is the willingness to take risks and to face challenges and obstacles with determination and fortitude. It requires a willingness to push beyond one's comfort zone and to embrace the unknown. Courage is a critical component of the warrior mindset, as it allows individuals to take on challenges with confidence and to pursue their goals with determination and purpose.

F. Integrity

Integrity is the quality of being honest and having strong moral principles. It requires a commitment to doing what is right, even in the face of adversity and opposition. Integrity is a critical component of the warrior mindset, as it allows individuals to remain true to themselves and to their values, even in the midst of difficult circumstances.

G. Perseverance

Perseverance is the ability to persist in the face of adversity and to keep going even when things get tough. It requires mental and emotional toughness, as well as a willingness to learn from mistakes and failures. Perseverance is a critical component of the warrior mindset, as it allows individuals to stay focused on their goals and to overcome obstacles and challenges with determination and persistence.

In summary, the key principles of the warrior mindset include self-discipline, resilience, adaptability, focus, courage, integrity, and perseverance. These principles form the foundation for success in all areas of life, and can be applied in a variety of contexts, from physical training and martial arts to personal and professional development. By embracing these principles, individuals can develop the mental and emotional resilience they need to succeed in the face of adversity and uncertainty.

A. Courage and fearlessness

Courage and fearlessness are key components of the warrior mindset. Courage is the willingness to take risks and to face challenges and obstacles with determination and fortitude. Fearlessness is the absence of fear, or the ability to push beyond one's comfort zone and to embrace the unknown.

In order to develop courage and fearlessness, individuals must first be willing to confront their fears. This requires a willingness to step outside of one's comfort zone and to take risks. It also requires a commitment to learning from one's mistakes and failures, and to using those experiences as opportunities for growth and development.

One way to develop courage and fearlessness is through exposure therapy. This involves gradually exposing oneself to situations that provoke fear or anxiety, in a controlled and supportive environment. Through this process, individuals can learn to manage their fear and anxiety, and to develop greater confidence and resilience.

Another important strategy for developing courage and fearlessness is through physical training and martial arts. By pushing oneself physically and mentally, individuals can develop greater confidence and resilience, and learn to push beyond their perceived limitations.

Ultimately, the development of courage and fearlessness requires a willingness to embrace the unknown, to take risks, and to confront one's fears. By doing so, individuals can develop the mental and emotional resilience they need to succeed in the face of adversity and uncertainty.

B. PERSEVERANCE AND RESILIENCE

Perseverance and resilience are essential principles of the warrior mindset. Perseverance is the ability to maintain one's efforts and focus in the face of adversity and setbacks, while resilience is the ability to recover from setbacks and bounce back from challenges.

To develop perseverance and resilience, individuals must first be willing to embrace the challenge of pursuing their goals and dreams. This requires a commitment to hard work, discipline, and dedication. It also requires a willingness to learn from setbacks and failures, and to use those experiences as opportunities for growth and development.

One key strategy for developing perseverance and resilience is to adopt a growth mindset. This involves the belief that one's abilities and talents can be developed through hard work and dedication, rather than being fixed and unchangeable. By adopting a growth mindset, individuals can approach challenges with a sense of curiosity and a willingness to learn, rather than with a fixed mindset that sees failure as a reflection of one's inherent limitations.

Another important strategy for developing perseverance and resilience is through physical training and martial arts. By pushing oneself physically and mentally, individuals can develop greater endurance, stamina, and mental toughness. This can help individuals to push beyond their perceived limitations and to develop the resilience they need to persevere through challenging times.

Ultimately, the development of perseverance and resilience requires a willingness to embrace the challenges and setbacks that come with pursuing one's goals and dreams. By doing so, individuals can develop the mental and emotional toughness they need to overcome obstacles and achieve success.

C. Honor and Integrity

Honor and integrity are core principles of the warrior mindset. Honor is the idea of living up to a set of values and principles, while integrity is the idea of consistently behaving in accordance with those values and principles.

To develop honor and integrity, individuals must first be willing to identify their core values and principles. This requires reflection and introspection, and a willingness to live up to a set of ideals that guide one's thoughts, words, and actions.

One key strategy for developing honor and integrity is to practice self-discipline and self-control. This involves developing the ability to regulate one's emotions and impulses, and to act in accordance with one's values and principles even in the face of temptation or pressure.

Another important strategy for developing honor and integrity is to practice honesty and transparency in one's relationships with others. This involves being truthful and straightforward in one's communication, and being willing to admit when one has made a mistake or fallen short of one's ideals.

Finally, practicing honor and integrity requires a willingness to take responsibility for one's actions and to be accountable for one's mistakes. This involves owning up to one's mistakes, apologizing when necessary, and making amends where possible.

Ultimately, the development of honor and integrity requires a commitment to living up to a set of values and principles, and a willingness to hold oneself accountable to those ideals. By doing so, individuals can develop a sense of personal integrity and self-respect, and earn the respect of others through their consistent adherence to their values and principles.

D. Compassion and Empathy

Compassion and empathy are important principles of the warrior mindset that are often overlooked or undervalued. While many people associate the warrior mindset with toughness and strength, true warriors understand that compassion and empathy are essential to their success.

Compassion is the ability to feel and show kindness, empathy, and concern for others, particularly those who are suffering. Empathy is the ability to understand and share the feelings of others. Together, these principles help warriors to develop a deep sense of connection and empathy with others, which can be a powerful source of motivation and strength.

To develop compassion and empathy, individuals must first be willing to cultivate a sense of humility and empathy. This involves being open to the experiences of others, and being willing to listen to their perspectives and insights. It also involves developing a sense of curiosity and wonder about the world around us, and being willing to learn from others.

One key strategy for developing compassion and empathy is to practice acts of kindness and generosity towards others. This involves doing things that show compassion, such as volunteering, donating to charity, or helping those in need. It also involves practicing empathy, by putting oneself in the shoes of others and seeking to understand their experiences and perspectives.

Another important strategy for developing compassion and empathy is to practice mindfulness and meditation. This involves developing a sense of inner calm and serenity, which can help individuals to be more present and attentive to the needs of others.

Ultimately, the development of compassion and empathy requires a willingness to connect with others on a deep and meaningful level. By doing so, individuals can develop a sense of purpose and motivation that goes beyond their own individual needs and desires, and find greater fulfillment and satisfaction in their lives.

E. Adaptability and flexibility

Adaptability and flexibility are essential principles of the warrior mindset that help individuals to respond to changing circumstances and overcome adversity. The ability to adapt and be flexible is crucial in any environment, but particularly in challenging and uncertain situations.

To develop adaptability and flexibility, individuals must first be willing to embrace change and uncertainty. This involves cultivating a sense of openness and curiosity, and being willing to explore new possibilities and approaches.

One key strategy for developing adaptability and flexibility is to practice resilience in the face of adversity. This involves developing the ability to bounce back from setbacks and challenges, and to maintain a positive outlook in the face of difficulty.

Another important strategy for developing adaptability and flexibility is to practice creativity and innovation. This involves being willing to experiment and take risks, and to think outside the box when facing challenges or problems.

Finally, practicing adaptability and flexibility requires a willingness to learn from one's experiences and to make adjustments as necessary. This involves being open to feedback and criticism, and being willing to make changes to one's approach when things are not working.

Ultimately, the development of adaptability and flexibility requires a commitment to ongoing learning and growth, and a willingness to embrace new experiences and challenges. By doing so, individuals can develop the skills and mindset needed to overcome adversity and achieve their goals, even in the face of uncertainty and change.

IV. APPLYING THE WARRIOR MINDSET TO REAL LIFE

The principles and strategies of the warrior mindset are not just theoretical concepts but can be applied to real-life situations to achieve success and personal growth. In this section, we will explore how the warrior mindset can be applied to different areas of life.

A. Career and Business

The warrior mindset can be particularly useful in the workplace, where individuals are required to navigate complex situations and overcome challenges. To apply the warrior mindset to one's career or business, individuals can focus on developing key skills such as resilience, focus, and adaptability.

By developing resilience, individuals can learn to bounce back from setbacks and challenges in their career. By building focus, individuals can maintain concentration and determination to achieve their goals. By developing adaptability, individuals can learn to be flexible and embrace new opportunities and challenges that arise.

B. Relationships

The warrior mindset can also be applied to relationships, where individuals must navigate complex interpersonal dynamics and communicate effectively. To apply the warrior mindset to relationships, individuals can focus on developing key skills such as empathy, compassion, and integrity.

By cultivating empathy and compassion, individuals can learn to understand and connect with others on a deeper level, building trust and mutual respect. By developing integrity, individuals can maintain honesty and transparency in their relationships, creating a foundation of trust and respect.

C. HEALTH AND WELLNESS

The warrior mindset can also be applied to health and wellness, where individuals must cultivate discipline and perseverance to achieve their goals. To apply the warrior mindset to health and wellness, individuals can focus on developing key skills such as discipline, focus, and perseverance.

By developing discipline, individuals can cultivate healthy habits and routines that support their physical and mental health. By building focus, individuals can maintain concentration and determination to achieve their health goals. By developing perseverance, individuals can maintain their commitment to their health goals even in the face of setbacks and challenges.

D. Personal Growth and Development

Finally, the warrior mindset can be applied to personal growth and development, where individuals seek to develop their full potential and achieve their highest aspirations. To apply the warrior mindset to personal growth and development, individuals can focus on developing key skills such as self-awareness, creativity, and adaptability.

By cultivating self-awareness, individuals can gain a deeper understanding of their strengths, weaknesses, and aspirations, and use this insight to guide their personal growth. By developing creativity, individuals can explore new possibilities and approaches to personal growth, breaking through self-imposed limitations. By developing adaptability, individuals can navigate the ever-changing landscape of personal growth and development, and overcome obstacles to achieve their highest aspirations.

V. CONCLUSION

In this book, we have explored the warrior mindset, its key principles, and strategies for applying it to real-life situations. By developing the warrior mindset, individuals can achieve greater success, personal growth, and fulfillment in their lives. Whether in their career, relationships, health, or personal development, the principles of the warrior mindset can be applied to achieve one's highest aspirations and potential. By embracing the warrior mindset, individuals can tap into their inner strength, resilience, and creativity, and overcome challenges to achieve success and personal growth.

A. Setting and achieving goals

Setting and achieving goals is a crucial aspect of the warrior mindset, as it requires discipline, focus, and perseverance. The process of setting and achieving goals can help individuals build their confidence, resilience, and sense of purpose, as they work towards achieving their aspirations.

To apply the warrior mindset to setting and achieving goals, individuals can follow the following steps:

Identify Your Goals:

The first step is to identify your goals and aspirations, and write them down. This process can help you clarify your priorities and create a clear plan for achieving your goals.

Break Down Your Goals into Smaller Steps:

Once you have identified your goals, break them down into smaller, more manageable steps. This will make your goals more achievable, and allow you to track your progress along the way.

Create a Plan:

Develop a plan of action for achieving your goals, including specific actions you can take to move closer to your goals each day. This plan should include a timeline and benchmarks for measuring progress.

Build Discipline:

Achieving your goals requires discipline and consistency. Build daily habits and routines that support your goals, and hold yourself accountable for staying on track.

Embrace Perseverance:

The road to achieving your goals is rarely smooth, and setbacks and challenges are inevitable. Embrace perseverance and use setbacks as an opportunity to learn, grow, and adjust your plan as needed.

Celebrate Your Progress:

As you make progress towards your goals, take time to celebrate your achievements and acknowledge your hard work and dedication. Celebrating your progress can boost your motivation and help you stay committed to achieving your goals.

By applying the warrior mindset to setting and achieving goals, individuals can develop the discipline, focus, and perseverance necessary to achieve their aspirations. This process can help individuals build confidence, resilience, and a sense of purpose, and achieve greater success and fulfillment in their lives.

B. Overcoming challenges and obstacles

Overcoming challenges and obstacles is a key aspect of the warrior mindset, as it requires courage, resilience, and adaptability. In life, we are often faced with unexpected challenges and obstacles that can derail us from our goals and aspirations. However, individuals who possess a warrior mindset have the tools and skills necessary to overcome these challenges and emerge stronger on the other side.

To apply the warrior mindset to overcoming challenges and obstacles, individuals can follow the following steps:

Reframe Your Perspective:

The first step is to reframe your perspective on the challenge or obstacle. Instead of viewing it as a roadblock, view it as an opportunity to learn, grow, and develop new skills. This can help shift your mindset from one of defeat to one of empowerment and growth.

Stay Positive:

Maintaining a positive mindset is key to overcoming challenges and obstacles. Focus on what you can control and take small, positive steps towards your goal each day. Celebrate your progress and stay optimistic about your ability to overcome the challenge.

Build Resilience:

Resilience is the ability to bounce back from setbacks and challenges. To build resilience, focus on developing a strong support system, practicing self-care, and staying committed to your goals and aspirations.

Embrace Adaptability:

The ability to adapt to changing circumstances is a key aspect of the warrior mindset. When faced with a challenge, be willing to adjust your approach and try new strategies. Embrace flexibility and remain open to new ideas and opportunities.

Take Action:

Overcoming challenges and obstacles requires action. Take small, intentional steps towards your goal each day and stay committed to your vision. Don't let fear or self-doubt hold you back. Instead, use your warrior mindset to push through and take action towards your goals.

By applying the warrior mindset to overcoming challenges and obstacles, individuals can develop the resilience, adaptability, and courage necessary to navigate life's challenges with confidence and grace. This process can help individuals build their self-esteem, develop new skills, and achieve greater success and fulfillment in their lives.

C. Building Strong Relationships and Networks

Building strong relationships and networks is another key area where the warrior mindset can be applied. Strong relationships and networks are essential for personal and professional growth, as they provide support, guidance, and opportunities for learning and development.

To apply the warrior mindset to building strong relationships and networks, individuals can follow the following steps:

Practice Communication Skills:

Communication is key to building strong relationships and networks. Practice active listening, speaking with clarity and conviction, and engaging in open, honest dialogue with others.

Show Respect and Compassion:

Respect and compassion are essential components of building strong relationships and networks. Show others that you value and care about their perspectives, opinions, and feelings.

Build Trust:

Trust is the foundation of strong relationships and networks. Be honest, reliable, and follow through on your commitments. Trust takes time to build, but it can be lost quickly if not nurtured and maintained.

Seek Out Mentors and Allies:

Mentors and allies can provide guidance, support, and opportunities for growth and development. Seek out individuals who share your values and aspirations and learn from their experiences and insights.

Give Back:

Giving back to others can help build strong relationships and networks. Offer support, advice, and assistance to others when you can, and be willing to lend a hand when someone else needs help.

By applying the warrior mindset to building strong relationships and networks, individuals can develop the interpersonal skills and emotional intelligence necessary to thrive in both their personal and professional lives. Strong relationships and networks can provide a sense of community, belonging, and purpose, and can help individuals achieve their goals and aspirations with greater ease and confidence.

D. Pursuing excellence in all areas of life

Pursuing excellence is a core tenet of the warrior mindset. It involves setting high standards for oneself and striving to meet or exceed those standards in all areas of life, from personal and professional development to relationships and health.

To apply the warrior mindset to pursuing excellence, individuals can follow the following steps:

Set Clear Goals:

Identify specific, measurable, achievable, relevant, and time-bound (SMART) goals in all areas of life. These goals should be challenging but realistic, and should reflect your core values and aspirations.

Develop a Plan:

Once you have identified your goals, develop a plan of action to achieve them. This plan should include specific steps, milestones, and deadlines, as well as a system for tracking progress and adjusting course as needed.

Cultivate a Growth Mindset:

A growth mindset involves a belief that one's abilities and intelligence can be developed over time with effort and persistence. Cultivate a growth mindset by embracing challenges, learning from failure, seeking out feedback, and focusing on the process rather than just the outcome.

Practice Continuous Improvement:

Pursuing excellence requires a commitment to ongoing learning and development. Seek out opportunities to learn new skills, acquire new knowledge, and expand your horizons. Read books, attend conferences and workshops, and engage in networking and mentoring relationships to accelerate your growth and development.

Prioritize Self-Care:

Pursuing excellence can be demanding and exhausting, so it is important to prioritize self-care. This includes getting enough sleep, eating a healthy diet, engaging in regular exercise, and taking breaks to recharge and refocus.

By applying the warrior mindset to pursuing excellence, individuals can achieve their goals and aspirations with greater focus, determination, and resilience. Pursuing excellence can also help individuals develop a sense of purpose, meaning, and fulfillment in all areas of life.

E. Making a positive impact on the world

Making a positive impact on the world is a powerful way to apply the warrior mindset to real life. It involves identifying opportunities to contribute to a greater good and using one's skills, resources, and influence to create positive change in the world.

To apply the warrior mindset to making a positive impact on the world, individuals can follow the following steps:

Identify Your Passion and Purpose:

Begin by identifying the causes, issues, or areas of interest that you are passionate about. Consider your personal experiences, values, and strengths, and reflect on the impact you would like to make on the world.

Develop Your Skills and Expertise:

To make a meaningful contribution, it is important to develop the skills and expertise needed to be effective in your chosen area of impact. Seek out opportunities to learn from experts in the field, participate in relevant training and education, and engage in hands-on experience and practice.

Find Your Role:

Making a positive impact on the world requires a team effort, so it is important to identify your role and niche in the larger ecosystem of change. Consider how your skills and expertise can best contribute to the larger effort, and seek out partners and collaborators who can help you achieve your goals.

Take Action:

Once you have identified your passion, purpose, and role, it is time to take action. This can involve volunteering, fundraising, advocating for policy change, building awareness and education, and more. It is important to set specific goals, develop a plan of action, and track progress to ensure you are making a meaningful impact.

Reflect and Adjust:

Making a positive impact on the world is an ongoing process, and it is important to reflect on your progress, adjust your strategy as needed, and continue learning and growing. Seek out feedback from others, reflect on your successes and failures, and make adjustments to your approach as needed to maximize your impact.

By applying the warrior mindset to making a positive impact on the world, individuals can create meaningful change in the world while also developing a sense of purpose, fulfillment, and contribution. Making a positive impact on the world is a powerful way to use one's skills, resources, and influence to make a difference in the world and leave a lasting legacy.

V. TOOLS AND TECHNIQUES FOR DEVELOPING THE WARRIOR MINDSET

Developing the warrior mindset is a lifelong journey that requires commitment, discipline, and practice. Fortunately, there are many tools and techniques that can help individuals cultivate the key traits and principles of the warrior mindset. Here are some of the most effective tools and techniques:

PHYSICAL TRAINING:

Physical training is a powerful way to develop physical and mental toughness, discipline, and resilience. Activities like martial arts, weightlifting, endurance training, and sports can help individuals push their limits and build strength, endurance, and confidence.

MENTAL TRAINING:

Mental training involves developing the ability to focus, concentrate, and manage emotions and thoughts effectively. Techniques like visualization, self-talk, goal-setting, and meditation can help individuals develop mental toughness, emotional intelligence, and a strong mindset.

Mindfulness:

Mindfulness involves cultivating awareness of the present moment, without judgment or distraction. By practicing mindfulness, individuals can develop greater self-awareness, self-regulation, and emotional resilience, and cultivate a sense of calm, clarity, and purpose.

Journaling:

Journaling is a powerful way to reflect on one's thoughts, emotions, and experiences, and gain insights into one's patterns, beliefs, and values. By regularly journaling, individuals can develop self-awareness, identify areas for growth and improvement, and clarify their goals and priorities.

COACHING AND MENTORING:

Coaching and mentoring involve seeking out guidance and support from experienced individuals who can provide guidance, feedback, and accountability. By working with coaches and mentors, individuals can accelerate their growth, develop new skills, and gain new perspectives and insights.

COMMUNITY AND SUPPORT NETWORKS:

Building a community of like-minded individuals who share one's values, goals, and aspirations can be a powerful source of support and motivation. By connecting with others who are on a similar journey, individuals can share resources, insights, and encouragement, and stay motivated and accountable.

By using these tools and techniques, individuals can cultivate the warrior mindset and develop the skills, traits, and principles needed to succeed in all areas of life. The key is to approach the journey with an open mind, a willingness to learn and grow, and a commitment to daily practice and discipline.

A. VISUALIZATION AND AFFIRMATIONS

Visualization and affirmations are powerful tools for developing the warrior mindset. Visualization involves creating mental images of oneself achieving a desired outcome, while affirmations involve repeating positive statements to oneself.

Visualization can help individuals develop greater self-confidence, motivation, and focus, by creating a clear mental picture of what they want to achieve. By visualizing themselves succeeding, individuals can build the belief and confidence that they can achieve their goals, and develop a stronger sense of purpose and direction. Visualization can also help individuals overcome fear and anxiety, by imagining themselves successfully navigating challenging situations.

Affirmations involve repeating positive statements to oneself, to reinforce a positive self-image and mindset. For example, an individual might repeat statements like "I am strong and resilient" or "I am capable of overcoming any challenge." By repeating these statements regularly, individuals can reprogram their subconscious mind to focus on positive beliefs and attitudes, and develop a stronger sense of self-worth and confidence.

To use visualization and affirmations effectively, it's important to:

Be specific:

Visualize and affirm a specific goal or outcome, with as much detail as possible.

Use the present tense:

Use language that suggests that the goal has already been achieved, to reinforce a sense of confidence and certainty.

Believe in the outcome: Visualization and affirmations are most effective when they are based on a genuine belief and desire for the outcome.

Repeat regularly:

Practice visualization and affirmations regularly, ideally on a daily basis, to reinforce positive beliefs and attitudes.

By using visualization and affirmations, individuals can develop a stronger sense of purpose, confidence, and self-belief, and cultivate the mindset needed to achieve their goals and succeed in all areas of life.

B. Mental Rehearsal and Preparation

Mental rehearsal and preparation are techniques that can help individuals develop the warrior mindset by visualizing and mentally preparing for challenges and opportunities in advance. By imagining oneself successfully navigating a challenging situation, individuals can develop greater confidence, focus, and resilience when facing similar situations in real life.

Mental rehearsal involves visualizing oneself performing a task or achieving a goal, as if it were actually happening in real life. This technique can be particularly effective for preparing for high-pressure situations, such as public speaking, athletic competitions, or job interviews. By mentally rehearsing the situation beforehand, individuals can reduce anxiety, boost self-confidence, and perform at their best when it matters most.

Mental preparation, on the other hand, involves developing a proactive and positive mindset towards upcoming challenges. This involves anticipating potential obstacles or setbacks, and mentally preparing oneself to handle them effectively. By focusing on the potential solutions and positive outcomes, individuals can develop a sense of control and preparedness, and be better equipped to handle whatever comes their way.

To use mental rehearsal and preparation effectively, it's important to:

Be specific:

Visualize and prepare for a specific situation or challenge, with as much detail as possible.

Stay positive:

Focus on positive outcomes and solutions, and avoid dwelling on potential negative outcomes.

Practice regularly:

Mental rehearsal and preparation are most effective when they are practiced regularly, ideally on a daily basis.

Stay flexible:

Be open to adjusting mental rehearsal and preparation techniques as circumstances change.

By using mental rehearsal and preparation techniques, individuals can develop a stronger sense of confidence, focus, and resilience, and be better equipped to handle challenges and opportunities in all areas of life.

C. POSITIVE SELF-TALK AND MINDSET SHIFTS

Positive self-talk and mindset shifts are powerful tools for developing the warrior mindset. By consciously cultivating positive thoughts and beliefs, individuals can boost their self-confidence, motivation, and resilience, and overcome limiting beliefs or negative self-talk that may hold them back.

Positive self-talk involves consciously replacing negative thoughts or self-talk with positive, empowering statements. For example, instead of telling oneself "I can't do this," one might reframe the thought as "I can do this, and I will figure it out." By consciously choosing positive, empowering statements, individuals can boost their self-confidence and motivation, and develop a more positive outlook on life.

Mindset shifts, on the other hand, involve consciously reframing one's perspective on a situation or challenge. This might involve seeing a setback or failure as an opportunity for growth and learning, or reframing a difficult situation as a challenge to be overcome rather than an insurmountable obstacle. By shifting one's mindset in this way, individuals can develop greater resilience, creativity, and flexibility, and be better equipped to handle challenges and opportunities in all areas of life.

To use positive self-talk and mindset shifts effectively, it's important to:

Be aware of negative self-talk or limiting beliefs:

Pay attention to the thoughts and beliefs that may be holding you back, and consciously work to replace them with positive, empowering statements.

Choose empowering statements:

Choose positive, empowering statements that resonate with you and help you feel confident and motivated.

Reframe challenges as opportunities:

Instead of seeing challenges or setbacks as failures, see them as opportunities for growth and learning, and approach them with a positive, solution-focused mindset.

Practice regularly:

Positive self-talk and mindset shifts are most effective when they are practiced regularly, ideally on a daily basis.

By using positive self-talk and mindset shifts, individuals can develop a stronger sense of confidence, motivation, and resilience, and be better equipped to handle challenges and opportunities in all areas of life.

D. Learning from failure and setbacks

Learning from failure and setbacks is a crucial tool for developing the warrior mindset. Failure and setbacks are an inevitable part of life, but they can be powerful opportunities for growth and learning, and a chance to build greater resilience, adaptability, and determination.

To learn from failure and setbacks, it's important to approach them with a growth mindset. This involves seeing failure and setbacks as opportunities for learning and growth, rather than as personal flaws or weaknesses. Rather than giving up or dwelling on the failure, individuals with a growth mindset will seek to understand what went wrong, and what they can do differently in the future to achieve their goals.

Some key strategies for learning from failure and setbacks include:

Take responsibility:

Own up to your mistakes and take responsibility for what went wrong. This will help you avoid making the same mistakes in the future and help you develop greater self-awareness.

Analyze what went wrong:

Take the time to reflect on what went wrong and identify the factors that contributed to the failure. This might involve talking to others, seeking feedback, or analyzing your own actions and thought processes.

Learn from your mistakes:

Once you've identified the factors that contributed to the failure, identify the lessons you can learn from the experience. This might involve identifying specific skills or knowledge gaps you need to address, or identifying patterns of behavior or thought that may be holding you back.

Reframe failure as feedback:

Rather than seeing failure as a personal failing, reframe it as feedback that can help you improve. By seeing failure in this way, you can approach it with a more positive, growth-oriented mindset.

Keep moving forward:

Once you've learned from your mistakes, use that knowledge to move forward and take new action towards your goals. Remember that setbacks and failures are an inevitable part of the journey, but they can also be powerful opportunities for growth and learning.

By learning from failure and setbacks, individuals can develop greater resilience, adaptability, and determination, and be better equipped to handle challenges and opportunities in all areas of life.

E. Continuous improvement and self-reflection

Continuous improvement and self-reflection are also important tools for developing the warrior mindset. By continually assessing one's strengths and weaknesses, setting goals, and taking action to improve, individuals can build greater self-awareness, self-discipline, and a growth mindset.

Some key strategies for continuous improvement and self-reflection include:

Set goals:

Identify specific, measurable, and achievable goals that align with your values and priorities. Write them down, and create a plan for achieving them.

Track progress:

Regularly track your progress towards your goals, and assess what's working and what's not. This can help you identify areas for improvement and adjust your approach as needed.

Seek feedback:

Ask for feedback from trusted sources, such as mentors, coaches, or colleagues. This can help you identify blind spots and areas for improvement that you may not be aware of.

Learn new skills and knowledge:

Identify skills and knowledge gaps that are holding you back, and take action to address them. This might involve taking classes, reading books, or seeking out mentorship or coaching.

Reflect on your actions and thought processes:

Regularly reflect on your actions and thought processes, and identify patterns that may be holding you back. This might involve journaling, meditation, or talking with a trusted friend or mentor.

By continuously striving to improve and reflect on their actions and thought processes, individuals can develop greater self-awareness, self-discipline, and a growth mindset. This can help them stay focused on their goals, navigate challenges and obstacles, and achieve success in all areas of life.

VI. THE WARRIOR MINDSET IN ACTION: INSPIRATIONAL STORIES AND EXAMPLES

The warrior mindset in action is exemplified by individuals who have demonstrated remarkable resilience, courage, and determination in the face of adversity. These inspirational stories and examples can serve as a source of motivation and inspiration for those seeking to develop their own warrior mindset.

Here are a few examples:

NELSON MANDELA:

Nelson Mandela's unwavering commitment to justice, peace, and equality despite 27 years in prison is a testament to his incredible courage, resilience, and perseverance. His ability to forgive his oppressors and work towards reconciliation has inspired people around the world.

SERENA WILLIAMS:

Serena Williams' success as a professional athlete is a testament to her mental toughness, perseverance, and commitment to continuous improvement. Despite facing racism and sexism throughout her career, she has become one of the most successful tennis players of all time.

MALALA YOUSAFZAI:

Malala Yousafzai's bravery in standing up for the education and rights of girls in Pakistan despite facing death threats from the Taliban is a testament to her incredible courage and determination. She has become a powerful advocate for human rights around the world.

JOCKO WILLINK:

Jocko Willink is a former Navy SEAL and author who has become a prominent advocate for the warrior mindset. His dedication to discipline, mental toughness, and self-improvement has inspired many to push themselves to new heights.

BETHANY HAMILTON:

Bethany Hamilton is a professional surfer who lost her arm in a shark attack at the age of 13. Her determination to continue surfing despite this setback, and her subsequent success as a professional athlete, is a testament to her resilience, courage, and perseverance.

MAYA ANGELOU:

Maya Angelou was an author, poet, and civil rights activist who overcame a traumatic childhood to become one of the most important writers of the 20th century. Her dedication to self-expression, self-improvement, and social justice is a testament to her incredible resilience and strength.

NICK VUJICIC:

Nick Vujicic was born without arms or legs, but he has become a successful motivational speaker and author who inspires people around the world. His dedication to perseverance, optimism, and self-acceptance is a testament to the power of the human spirit.

TOM BRADY:

Tom Brady is one of the most successful football players of all time, but his success is not just due to his physical talent. His dedication to mental toughness, discipline, and continuous improvement is a testament to his incredible work ethic and drive.

HARRIET TUBMAN:

Harriet Tubman was a slave who escaped to freedom and then returned to the South to help other slaves escape via the Underground Railroad. Her incredible courage, determination, and commitment to justice and equality are a testament to the warrior mindset.

STEPHEN HAWKING:

Stephen Hawking was a renowned physicist and cosmologist who continued to work and make groundbreaking discoveries despite being diagnosed with ALS at the age of

21. His dedication to perseverance, curiosity, and innovation is a testament to his incredible intellect and spirit.

OPRAH WINFREY:

Oprah Winfrey is one of the most successful media personalities of all time, but her success is not just due to her talent. Her dedication to personal growth, self-improvement, and social justice is a testament to her incredible resilience and compassion.

BRUCE LEE:

Bruce Lee was a legendary martial artist and actor who popularized kung fu and became an icon of physical fitness and mental discipline. His dedication to continuous improvement, self-expression, and mindfulness is a testament to his incredible philosophy and mindset.

HELEN KELLER:

Helen Keller was deaf and blind from the age of 19 months, but she overcame these disabilities to become a prominent writer, activist, and speaker. Her dedication to communication, education, and social justice is a testament to her incredible resilience and spirit.

WINSTON CHURCHILL:

Winston Churchill was the Prime Minister of the United Kingdom during World War II, and his leadership and courage helped to lead the country to victory. His dedication to courage, perseverance, and resilience in the face of overwhelming odds is a testament to his incredible strength and leadership.

MICHAEL JORDAN:

Michael Jordan is one of the most successful basketball players of all time, but his success is not just due to his physical talent. His dedication to mental toughness, discipline, and self-improvement is a testament to his incredible work ethic and mindset.

These individuals and many others demonstrate the power of the warrior mindset in action. By embodying the key principles of the warrior mindset, they have been able to overcome incredible challenges and achieve remarkable success in their lives. Their stories serve as a powerful reminder that anyone can develop the warrior mindset and achieve their goals, no matter what obstacles they may face.

A. HISTORICAL FIGURES AND LEGENDARY WARRIORS

Miyamoto Musashi

a legendary samurai and warrior who became known as the greatest swordsman in Japanese history.

Sun Tzu

a Chinese general and military strategist who authored the famous book "The Art of War".

Alexander the Great

a king and military commander who conquered much of the ancient world and is still celebrated as one of history's greatest military minds.

Joan of Arc

a French heroine and military leader who played a pivotal role in the Hundred Years' War and was canonized as a saint.

William Wallace

a Scottish knight and leader of the Scottish forces during the Wars of Scottish Independence, known for his bravery and leadership.

Spartacus

a gladiator and leader of a slave rebellion against the Roman Republic, who inspired generations of revolutionaries.

Genghis Khan

a Mongolian emperor and military leader who founded the Mongol Empire, one of the largest empires in history.

Bruce Lee

a martial artist, actor, and philosopher who popularized martial arts in the Western world and inspired generations of martial artists.

Leonidas I

a Spartan king who led a small force of Greek soldiers against the Persian army at the Battle of Thermopylae, and became a symbol of bravery and sacrifice.

Saladin

a Muslim general who fought against the Crusaders in the Middle Ages and became renowned for his chivalry, generosity, and military prowess.

Lapu-Lapu

a chieftain of Mactan Island who defeated Ferdinand Magellan in the Battle of Mactan in 1521, and is regarded as the first Filipino hero. A legendary warrior who, according to folklore, possessed superhuman strength and was invulnerable to weapons.

Gabriela Silang

a Filipina revolutionary leader who fought against Spanish colonialism in the 18th century and became a symbol of women's bravery and leadership.

Andres Bonifacio

a founder and leader of the Katipunan, a revolutionary organization that fought against Spanish and later American colonial rule in the Philippines.

Emilio Aguinaldo

a revolutionary leader who declared the independence of the Philippines from Spanish colonialism in 1898, and became the country's first president.

Kudaman

a legendary warrior from the T'boli people of Mindanao, known for his bravery, strength, and wisdom.

Lam-ang

a legendary hero from the Ilocano epic "Biag ni Lam-ang", who possessed incredible strength and defeated numerous monsters and enemies.

Rajah Sulayman

a Muslim chieftain of Manila who resisted Spanish colonization in the 16th century and defended the city against invaders.

Francisco Balagtas

a poet and revolutionary who wrote the epic poem "Florante at Laura", which became a symbol of resistance against Spanish colonialism.

Gregorio del Pilar

a general who fought in the Philippine Revolution and later in the Philippine-American War, and became known for his bravery and sacrifice in the Battle of Tirad Pass.

Melchora Aquino

also known as Tandang Sora, she was a Filipina revolutionary who supported the Katipunan, and is known as the "Mother of the Philippine Revolution".

Marcelo H. del Pilar

a writer and journalist who fought against Spanish colonialism through his writings and publications, and became known as the "Father of Philippine Journalism".

Jose Rizal

a writer and revolutionary who is regarded as the national hero of the Philippines, and is known for his novels "Noli Me Tangere" and "El Filibusterismo", which exposed the injustices of Spanish colonialism.

Apolinario Mabini

a revolutionary leader and intellectual who served as the first prime minister of the Philippines, and is known as the "Sublime Paralytic" due to his physical disability.

Juan Luna

a painter and revolutionary who fought against Spanish colonialism and is known for his painting "Spoliarium", which won a gold medal in the Exposition Universelle in Paris.

Antonio Luna

a general and military strategist who fought in the Philippine Revolution and the Philippine-American War, and is known for his tactical brilliance and fiery personality.

Sultan Kudarat

a Muslim leader who fought against Spanish colonialism in Mindanao and is known for his bravery and leadership.

Francisco Dagohoy

a Boholano leader who led a rebellion against Spanish colonialism for over 80 years, and is known as the "Longest Revolution in Philippine History".

B. Modern-day martial artists and athletes

Here are some modern-day martial artists and athletes who exemplify the warrior mindset:

Ronda Rousey

a retired mixed martial artist and Olympic medalist who overcame numerous obstacles to become one of the most successful fighters in history.

Georges St-Pierre

a retired mixed martial artist who is widely considered to be one of the greatest fighters of all time, known for his focus, discipline, and mental toughness.

Anderson Silva

a retired mixed martial artist who held the UFC middleweight title for a record-breaking 2,457 days and is known for his incredible striking skills and calm under pressure.

Manny Pacquiao

a Filipino professional boxer who has won world championships in eight different weight divisions and is known for his incredible work ethic, discipline, and perseverance.

Simone Biles

an American artistic gymnast who has won numerous Olympic and World Championship medals and is known for her incredible mental and physical strength, as well as her ability to overcome setbacks and challenges.

Usain Bolt

a retired Jamaican sprinter who is widely considered to be the greatest sprinter of all time and known for his incredible speed, focus, and mental toughness.

Conor McGregor

an Irish mixed martial artist and boxer who is known for his incredible confidence, mental toughness, and ability to rise to the occasion in high-pressure situations.

Efren Reyes

A professional pool player who is widely considered to be one of the greatest of all time, Reyes is known for his incredible focus and mental toughness. He has won numerous international championships throughout his career.

Hidilyn Diaz

A weightlifter who made history by winning the Philippines' first-ever Olympic gold medal in the 2020 Tokyo Olympics. Diaz's success is a testament to her incredible strength, discipline, and perseverance.

Rolando Navarette

A former professional boxer who became the WBC super featherweight champion in 1981. Navarette was known for his aggressive style and relentless determination in the ring.

Monico Puentevella

A former competitive swimmer who represented the Philippines in numerous international competitions. Despite facing significant challenges and setbacks throughout his career, Puentevella persevered and became one of the most successful swimmers in Philippine history.

Rener and Ryron Gracie

These brothers are the grandsons of Brazilian Jiu-Jitsu pioneer Carlos Gracie, and are known for their expertise in the art of Brazilian Jiu-Jitsu. They have dedicated their lives to spreading the teachings of their family's martial art throughout the world.

Margarito "Ting" Toledo

A renowned coach and trainer who has produced numerous world-class fighters in various combat sports. Toledo is known for his dedication to his craft and his ability to instill the warrior mindset in his students.

Elorde brothers

Gabriel "Flash" Elorde and Juanito "Kid" Elorde are both Filipino boxing legends who were known for their speed, skill, and toughness in the ring. Gabriel was a former world champion and was inducted into the International Boxing Hall of Fame, while Juanito became a successful promoter and trainer.

Monsour Del Rosario

A former Taekwondo champion who won numerous international competitions throughout his career. Del Rosario is also an actor and stuntman, and has dedicated his life to promoting the martial arts in the Philippines.

Eduard Folayang

A former ONE Championship lightweight champion and mixed martial artist who is known for his incredible resilience and perseverance. Despite facing numerous setbacks and defeats throughout his career, Folayang has never given up on his dreams of becoming a world champion.

C. Everyday people who have applied the warrior mindset to succeed in life

There are many inspiring stories of Filipinos who have risen from rags to riches through hard work, determination, and the application of a warrior mindset.

Here are some examples:

Henry Sy

Born to a poor family in China, Sy migrated to the Philippines and started out as a shoe salesman. He went on to build one of the largest retail empires in Asia, SM Investments Corporation.

Manny Villar

Villar was born into poverty and had to help his family sell seafood to make ends meet. He worked hard, earned a degree in business administration, and went on to become a successful businessman, founding Vista Land & Lifescapes, Inc.

Tony Tan Caktiong

Caktiong started out with a small ice cream parlor in the Philippines and turned it into a multinational fast-food chain, Jollibee Foods Corporation.

Socorro Ramos

Known as the "National Bookstore Lady," Ramos started out with a small stall selling textbooks and school supplies in Manila. She grew her business into a chain of over 200 bookstores across the Philippines.

Teresita Sy-Coson

The daughter of Henry Sy, Sy-Coson is the current chairman of SM Investments

Corporation. She started out working in her father's department store and worked her way up the corporate ladder.

Gina Lopez

was an environmentalist and philanthropist who served as the chairperson of ABS-CBN Foundation. She helped launch several successful programs for the poor, including Bantay Bata 163 and Bantay Kalikasan.

Nanette Medved-Po

Medved-Po is a former actress who founded the social enterprise Hope in a Bottle. The company sells purified water and donates a portion of its profits to build classrooms in public schools.

Efren Peñaflorida

Peñaflorida is a teacher and social worker who founded the Dynamic Teen Company. The group provides education and training to street children in the Philippines.

Lea Salonga

Salonga is a singer and actress who started out performing in Manila theater productions. She went on to become an international star, winning a Tony Award for her role in the musical "Miss Saigon."

VII. CONCLUSION

The warrior mindset is a powerful philosophy that can help individuals overcome challenges, achieve their goals, and make a positive impact on the world. It involves developing physical and mental resilience, as well as cultivating key principles such as courage, perseverance, and compassion. By applying the warrior mindset to different aspects of their lives, individuals can improve their relationships, pursue excellence, and create a better future for themselves and others.

The journey of developing the warrior mindset is not easy, but it is worth it. It requires dedication, discipline, and a willingness to learn and grow. However, with the right tools and techniques, as well as inspiration from the stories of historical figures, modern-day athletes, and everyday people who have succeeded in life, anyone can develop the warrior mindset.

This book has explored the definition and importance of the warrior mindset, as well as its foundation, key principles, and application to real-life situations. It has also provided tools and techniques for developing the warrior mindset and examples of how it has been used by historical figures, modern-day martial artists and athletes, and ordinary people who have achieved success in their lives.

The warrior mindset is a philosophy that can benefit anyone, regardless of their background, profession, or goals. By developing the warrior mindset, individuals can cultivate the strength, discipline, and compassion needed to succeed in life and make a positive impact on the world.

A. Recap of key points

In this book, we explored the warrior mindset, an approach to life that draws inspiration from the principles and practices of martial arts and warrior cultures. We discussed the importance of developing the warrior mindset for success in life and examined the foundation and key principles of this mindset. We also provided practical advice on how to apply the warrior mindset to real life, as well as tools and techniques for developing this mindset. Finally, we explored inspirational stories and examples of historical figures, legendary warriors, modern-day martial artists and athletes, and everyday people who have applied the warrior mindset to succeed in life.

The key points of the book are as follows:

The warrior mindset is a set of attitudes and behaviors that are characterized by physical and mental toughness, discipline, focus, and mindfulness.

Developing the warrior mindset is important for success in all areas of life, including business, education, sports, and personal growth.

The foundation of the warrior mindset includes physical fitness and training, mental toughness and discipline, focus and concentration, and mindfulness and meditation.

The key principles of the warrior mindset include courage and fearlessness, perseverance and resilience, honor and integrity, compassion and empathy, and adaptability and flexibility.

Applying the warrior mindset to real life involves setting and achieving goals, overcoming challenges and obstacles, building strong relationships and networks, pursuing excellence in all areas of life, and making a positive impact on the world.

Tools and techniques for developing the warrior mindset include visualization and affirmations, mental rehearsal and preparation, positive self-talk and mindset shifts, learning from failure and setbacks, and continuous improvement and self-reflection.

Inspirational stories and examples of historical figures, legendary warriors, modern-day martial artists and athletes, and everyday people who have applied the warrior mindset to succeed in life can provide valuable insights and motivation.

The warrior mindset is a powerful and transformative approach to life that can help individuals achieve their goals, overcome challenges, and make a positive impact on the world. By cultivating physical and mental resilience, developing key principles such as courage, perseverance, and compassion, and applying these principles to real life, anyone can develop the warrior mindset and succeed in life.

B. Final thoughts and advice for readers

In conclusion, the warrior mindset is a powerful tool for achieving success in all areas of life. It is a mindset that requires discipline, mental toughness, and a commitment to continuous improvement. Through physical training, mental conditioning, and the cultivation of key principles such as courage, perseverance, honor, compassion, and adaptability, individuals can develop the warrior mindset and achieve their goals.

The book has provided an overview of the warrior mindset, its importance, key principles, and practical applications in real life. It has also outlined tools and techniques for developing the warrior mindset, as well as examples of historical figures, legendary warriors, modern-day martial artists and athletes, and ordinary people who have applied the warrior mindset to succeed in life.

For readers who are interested in developing the warrior mindset, my advice is to start by setting clear goals and developing a plan of action for achieving them. This could include a physical fitness routine, a meditation practice, and a commitment to continuous learning and self-improvement. It is also important to stay focused, remain adaptable, and surround oneself with positive influences and supportive networks.

Above all, the warrior mindset is about embracing a life of purpose and making a positive impact on the world. By living with honor, integrity, compassion, and a commitment to excellence, individuals can achieve great things and leave a lasting legacy.

C. CALL TO ACTION FOR DEVELOPING THE WARRIOR MINDSET AND ACHIEVING SUCCESS IN LIFE

In conclusion, the warrior mindset is a powerful tool for achieving success in life. By combining physical and mental fitness, focus and concentration, mindfulness and meditation, courage and fearlessness, perseverance and resilience, honor and integrity, compassion and empathy, adaptability and flexibility, individuals can develop a mindset that is geared towards success.

The key principles of the warrior mindset include courage, perseverance, honor, compassion, and adaptability. By applying these principles to real-life situations such as goal setting, overcoming challenges, building strong relationships, pursuing excellence, and making a positive impact on the world, individuals can achieve success in all areas of life.

The book has provided tools and techniques for developing the warrior mindset, including visualization and affirmations, mental rehearsal and preparation, positive self-talk and mindset shifts, learning from failure and setbacks, and continuous improvement and self-reflection. These techniques can help individuals stay focused, motivated, and resilient in the face of challenges.

Inspirational stories and examples from historical figures, legendary warriors, modern-day martial artists and athletes, and everyday people who have applied the warrior mindset to succeed in life have been shared. Filipino examples of historical figures and legendary warriors, modern-day martial artists and athletes, and everyday people who have applied the warrior mindset to succeed in life have been shared as well.

As a final thought, developing the warrior mindset is not an easy feat, but with perseverance and determination, it is achievable. The book has provided readers with the tools, principles, and examples necessary for developing the warrior mindset and achieving success in life. Therefore, it is important for readers to take action and apply the knowledge and techniques presented in the book to their own lives. With a warrior mindset, individuals can overcome obstacles and achieve their dreams.

Printed in Great Britain
by Amazon